To the Reader . . .

"World Cities" focuses on cities as a way to learn about the major civilizations of the world. Each civilization has at its roots the life of one or more cities. Learning about life in the great cities is essential to understanding the past and present of the world and its people.

People live in cities for many reasons. For one thing, they value what cities can offer them culturally. Culture thrives in all cities. It is expressed in visual arts, music, and ethnic celebrations. In fact, a city's greatness is often measured by the richness of culture that it offers those who live there.

Many people choose to live in cities for economic reasons. Cities offer a variety of jobs and other economic opportunities. Many city dwellers have found prosperity through trade. Nearly all the world's great cities were founded on trade—the voluntary exchange of goods and services between people. The great cities remain major economic centers.

City living can, of course, have its disadvantages. Despite these disadvantages, cities continue to thrive. By reading about the people, culture, geography, and economy of various metropolitan centers, you will understand why. You will also understand why the world is becoming more and more urban. Finally, you will learn what it is that makes each world city unique.

Mark Schug, Consulting Editor
Co-author of *Teaching Social Studies in the Elementary School* and *Community Study*

CONSULTING EDITOR
Mark C. Schug
Professor of Curriculum and Instruction
University of Wisconsin-Milwaukee

EDITORIAL
Amy Bauman, Project Editor
Barbara J. Behm
Judith Smart, Editor-in-Chief

ART/PRODUCTION
Suzanne Beck, Art Director
Carole Kramer, Designer
Thom Pharmakis, Photo Researcher
Eileen Rickey, Typesetter
Andrew Rupniewski, Production Manager

Reviewed for accuracy by:
M. Eugene Gilliom
Professor of Social Studies Education
Ohio State University

Monica Thomas
Head of the Department of Economics
University of Alaska, Fairbanks

Library of Congress Number: 89-10393

3 4 5 6 7 8 9   96 95 94 93 92

Library of Congress Cataloging in Publication Data

Davis, James E., 1940-
  Moscow.
  (World cities)

  Summary: Explores the history, cultural heritage, demographics, geography, and economic and natural resources of Moscow.
  1. Moscow (R.S.F.S.R.)—Juvenile literature. [1. Moscow (R.S.F.S.R.)] I. Hawke, Sharryl Davis. II. Title. III. Series: Davis, James E., 1940- . World cities.
DK601.2.D38 1989 947′.312   [B] [92]   89-10393
ISBN 0-8172-3030-0 (lib. bdg.)

Cover Photo: Gamma / Liaison

MOSCOW

WORLD CITIES

JAMES E. DAVIS
AND
SHARRYL DAVIS HAWKE

RAINTREE
STECK-VAUGHN
L I B R A R Y

Austin, Texas

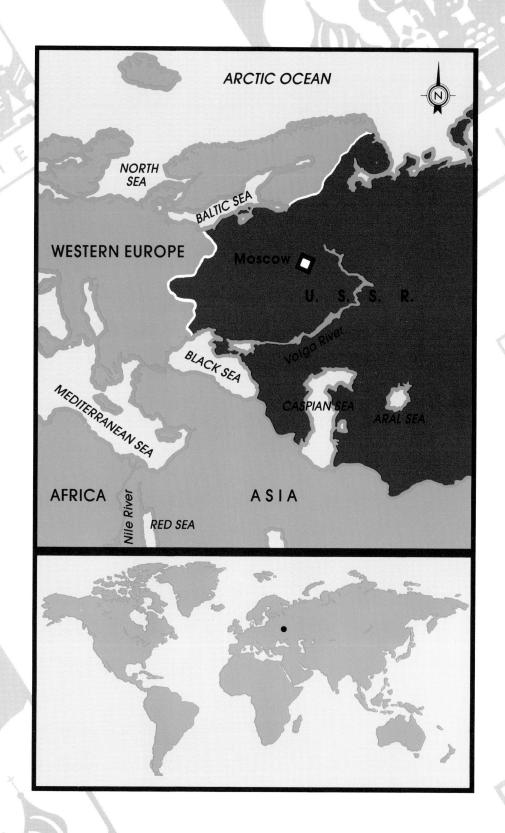

Contents

Introduction

Arriving at or departing from Moscow, an air traveler looks down on a city that appears to be built in the shape of a wheel. Two circular boulevards form inner and outer rims, and streets fan out from the center like spokes. The shape reflects the way the city grew outward from the Kremlin, a three-sided fortress that is as ancient as Moscow itself.

The Kremlin faces Red Square, the city's hub. Also facing Red Square are St. Basil's Cathedral, with its eight onion-shaped domes; the Russia Hotel, which is the largest in the world; and a huge department store called GUM.

Moscow, a city of nine million people spread over 400 square miles (1,040 square kilometers), is the capital of the Union of Soviet Socialist Republics (Soviet Union), one of the world's largest nations. The Kremlin is the center of government, where many workers and top officials have offices. The city is located in the western part of the Soviet Union, where the nation once known as Russia began about one thousand years ago. Moscow is also the capital of the Russian Soviet Federated Socialist Republic, the largest of the fifteen republics into which the country is divided.

More than one hundred different ethnic groups make up the Soviet Union's population of nearly 290 million people. Each group has its own language or dialect, traditions, and customs. The major groups include

St. Basil's Cathedral, with its eight colorful domes, faces Red Square in the heart of Moscow.

7

The Soviet Union is home to many ethnic groups. Tajiks—people from Soviet Central Asia—make up one such group (top). The Kremlin serves as the center of government. Workers sweep the streets there each morning (bottom).

Russians, Ukrainians, Byelorussians, Uzbeks, Armenians, Azerbaijanis, Turkmen, Georgians, Estonians, Latvians, and Lithuanians. One ethnic group forms the majority in each of the fifteen republics, and in the Russian Republic, nine out of ten people are Russian.

Like other cities that have existed for centuries, Moscow features contrasts between the old and the new. Red Square, for example, is paved with cobblestones, while streets radiating out from it have smooth surfaces. St. Basil's and other old churches stand against tall, modern office and apartment buildings. Crafts people use their skills in small, out-of-the-way shops, while huge factories produce automobiles and other goods. The Bolshoi Theater presents ballets composed two hundred years ago and yet also houses up-to-date movie theaters. Elderly women sweep Red Square and the streets around it with wooden brooms. Meanwhile, teenagers dressed in jeans and T-shirts stroll by, soft drinks in their hands, with radios tuned to rock music.

Moscow began as a small trading post on the Moscow River. Today it is one of the world's largest and most important cities.

WORLD CITIES

Early Moscow

At some time early in the 1100s, a fur trapper named Kuchka claimed the rise of land along the banks of the Moscow River as his own. He called the land he claimed Kuchkovo. From there he could move south down the Moscow to the Oka River, then east to meet the mighty Volga River. The Volga took him to the Caspian Sea, far to the south.

From the Moscow, Kuchka could also reach the Dnieper River to the west by portaging, which means dragging or carrying a boat a short distance across land from one waterway to another. The Dnieper flows south into the Black Sea. Kuchka could also link up with the Dvina River if he wished to go north to the Baltic Sea.

For many years before Kuchka made his claim, waterways and portages had formed an important north-south trade route through the land known as Russia. Traders moved along the route from the Baltic Sea to the city of Constantinople (now Istanbul) near the Black Sea. They carried furs, precious stones, jewelry, and many other goods.

The Founding of Moscow

In the year 1147, Yuri Dolgoruki, a young prince, saw the pine-covered hill by the Moscow River. The prince realized that he could journey from this site to many of Russia's major rivers. He could also travel to the seas. He knew that from this spot, he could defend himself against enemy armies.

The city of Moscow is built on the banks of the Moscow River. This spot is the very same spot on which Yuri Dolgoruki founded his original city in 1147.

Best of all, he knew that this spot could become a great center for trade. For all these reasons, Prince Dolgoruki wanted Kuchka's land. He is said to have murdered Kuchka to get the prized location.

In the center of Moscow today, there is a large statue of a man wearing a cape and a helmet. He is seated on a great prancing horse. The statue is of Yuri Dolgoruki. This bold prince is considered the city's founder.

The prince built a fort and a block-house to protect his new village, named Moscow after the river. The fort covered a little more than 2 acres (0.8 hectares). Today, the Kremlin occupies that very spot. The word *kreml* means "fort" in Russian, and today's Kremlin is much larger than Prince Dolgoruki's fort. It covers about 70 acres (28 ha), which is about the size of fifty-three football fields.

Despite the fort, enemy armies captured Moscow in 1237. The invaders were people called Mongols and Tatars, and they were from Central Asia. Their paths of conquest led south from their lands into China and west to eastern Europe, including Russia.

The Mongol-Tatar period in Russia lasted until late in the 1400s. During that time, the citizens of Moscow and elsewhere in Russia had to pay tribute in the form of money, furs, and other goods to their conquerors. If tribute was not paid, Mongol-Tatar soldiers would sweep in to enforce payment, burning villages and killing the Russian people.

As long as the people paid tribute, however, they could do as they pleased.

Moscow continued as a busy and prosperous trading center. Traders from present-day Sweden, Norway, and Finland visited the city to trade furs. Other traders came from the south with jewelry, fine wines, and silk cloth. Centuries later, workers digging a hole for a Moscow swimming pool found two ancient Arabian coins. This suggests that people from as far away as Arab countries, or people who had been trading in Arab countries, also came to Moscow in order to trade.

Mongol armies captured Moscow in 1237, and the Russian people were forced to make payments to the Mongol leaders. Finally, in 1380, Prince Dmitry of Moscow refused the Mongol's demands (below).

In the year 1366, Prince Dmitry of Moscow began to build a wall of white stone around the town to protect it against the Mongols and Tatars. Then, in 1380, his army defeated those enemies in battle, marking the first time anyone had accomplished that. However, Mongol-Tatar forces burned Moscow, and two years later recaptured it. Still, they had been defeated once, and might be again.

As the Muscovites rebuilt their town, the people of other towns and villages throughout Russia began to look to Moscow for leadership. The prince of the Moscow region also came to rule the principalities of Kiev to the southwest and Novgorod to the northwest.

The Russian Orthodox Church, an offshoot of the Greek Orthodox Church, had begun in Kiev in 988. In the 1300s, the head of the Russian Orthodox Church moved his residence to Moscow. That made Moscow the religious center for all the people of Russia.

Early Orthodox churches in Moscow were made of wood. The first white stone church was built in 1326, and later, the Cathedral of the Assumption was built on the same site. The cathedral was finished in 1479

Moscow is the seat of the Russian Orthodox Church. Today, this religion is the largest in the Soviet Union.

and still stands in the Kremlin. It is now open to the public as a national museum.

Finally, in 1480, the prince of the Moscow region, Ivan III, refused to pay any more tribute to the Mongols and Tatars. The Mongols and Tatars were weak by then and did not challenge him. This spelled the end of their dominance in Russia. Thus, Ivan III became the ruler of a vast area of land. Moscow was the central city of this new Russian Empire.

Moscow Under the Early Czars

After ridding the land of Mongols and Tatars, Prince Ivan III was called Ivan the Great. He adopted the two-headed eagle as his symbol, and this later became the symbol of the whole Russian Empire.

Finished in 1479, the Cathedral of the Assumption still stands inside the Kremlin walls.

James Pozarik / Gamma-Liaison

temper and the large number of people he had put to death as enemies. In one fit of rage, he killed his own son. Ivan IV is also known as the czar who opened exploration of Siberia, the vast area north and east of the empire. In addition, it was Ivan IV who opened trade with England through the Muscovy Company in 1555.

Ivan IV was also responsible for creating serfdom in the Russian Em-

The Bell Tower of Ivan the Great was built as the Kremlin's main watchtower (left). The Czar Cannon bears the likeness of Fyodor, son of Ivan the Terrible, on its side (below).

Click / Chicago Ltd. — D.E. Cox

Ivan III was the first ruler to call himself czar of all Russia. However, Ivan IV was the first to actually be crowned czar, or emperor. This ceremony took place in 1547 in the Kremlin's Cathedral of the Assumption. This beautiful old church with golden domes still contains the carved throne of Ivan IV.

Ivan IV later became known as Ivan the Terrible because of his murderous

pire. Before Ivan's rule, many of the Russian people were peasants. The peasants were a class of farmers and farm laborers. Although some peasants owned the land they worked and were well off, most were poor. However, all peasants had the freedom to move to new land or to the towns and cities. This system did not please the wealthy landowners. These landowners, or nobles, wanted workers on whom they could depend.

To aid the nobles, Ivan IV created serfdom. Many serfs came from a group called state peasants. These peasants paid fees and taxes directly to the czar. When the czar wished to reward army leaders, nobles, or other favorites, he gave them state peasants. The peasants then became serfs. Under this system, serfs belonged to the land. Landowners could sell their serfs or rent out their services. If the land was sold, the serfs were included in the sale. For the most part, serfs led miserable lives.

Over the centuries, the number of Russian serfs grew into the millions. Russia's whole economic system depended on these workers. For this reason, serfdom continued to exist until

Ivan IV was the first prince of Moscow to actually be crowned as czar of the Russians. Ivan's cruelty earned him the name "Ivan the Terrible."

The Bettmann Archive Inc.

1861. In that year, Czar Alexander II freed all serfs from service.

That event took place nearly three hundred years after the death of the cruel Ivan in 1584. A period known as the "Time of Troubles" followed Ivan's death. During this period, the empire was in a state of turmoil and civil war. The period finally ended in 1613, when Michael Romanov became

Russia was ruled by czars of the Romanov family from 1613 to 1917. Here, Czar Alexander II, one of the Romanov czars, crowns his wife as czarina in 1855.

were bakers and picklers, coachmen, soldiers, and such skilled workers as blacksmiths, tailors, jewelers, and printers. Factories produced firearms, gunpowder, cloth, and bricks.

The two hundred-ton Czar Bell is the biggest bell in the world (left). A piece weighing eleven tons broke off the bell when it was damaged in the Moscow fire of 1737. Czar Alexander II was the ruler who put an end to Russia's serfdom (below).

the first Romanov czar. The Romanov family was to rule for just over three hundred years.

The empire continued to expand into Siberia, southward to the Caspian and Black seas, and westward from Moscow. By the year 1700, Moscow was the triumphant capital of an energetic empire. Its population of 100,000 made it one of Europe's biggest cities. The population was made up of crafts people, traders, government officials, clergymen, nobles, and servants. There

WORLD CITIES

Growth of the City

At the beginning of the 1700s, the czar of Russia was a towering man named Peter I. This czar was also known as Peter the Great. He ruled Russia from 1682 to 1725. Among other things, Peter the Great is remembered for having moved the capital from Moscow in 1712.

Peter the Great moved the capital to a new city he had built where the Neva River flows into the Baltic Sea. He named the city St. Petersburg, and it was known as Russia's "window to the west." Today this city is called Leningrad.

Even though Moscow was no longer the capital after 1712, it was still an important city for trade and industry. Then, when Moscow University was founded in 1755, the city began to become important as a cultural center as well. The university trained scientists, doctors, and teachers. Theater and the arts also began to contribute to culture in Moscow in the 1700s. The first Russian theater and the Academy of Fine Arts were begun in 1756 and 1757, respectively.

The Defeat of Napoleon

Alexander I was czar as the 1800s began. At the same time, Napoleon I was emperor of France. Napoleon planned to conquer all of Europe, including Russia, and in 1812, he led his army of 600,000 into that country. Napoleon was determined to take Moscow.

French and Russian armies met at

the village of Borodino, outside of Moscow. Tens of thousands of soldiers died in the Battle of Borodino, and the Russians were forced to retreat into Moscow. From there the Russian army, along with most residents of the city, moved toward the east.

Napoleon camped on a hill two miles from Moscow, waiting for the Russians to send officials to surrender. No one came. Napoleon sent scouts into Moscow, who reported that the city was deserted.

Peter the Great, at left, moved Russia's capital from Moscow to St. Petersburg (now known as Leningrad) in 1712. Still, Moscow continued to be an important city, and Moscow University was founded there in 1755 (below).

When Napoleon's army captured Moscow in 1812, they found it deserted. Soon after, a mysterious fire destroyed the city.

The French Army moved in, bothered only by a few musket shots, and Napoleon set up his headquarters in the Kremlin. But a few nights later, the whole city suddenly went up in flames. The raging fire consumed three out of every four buildings, which burned quickly because they were made of wood. The glow of flames could be seen from 60 miles (96 km) away.

Moscow burned for six days, from September 3 to September 8, 1812. No one knows for sure who set the fires, but it may have been the Russians themselves, hoping to drive Napoleon from their city. In any case, there was nothing left to eat and little shelter when the flames died out.

By October 7, 1812, Napoleon's army had used up all its food supplies. Winter was coming. Still there was no Russian surrender. Napoleon finally gave up, but as his army left the city, troops fired a few last cannon shots. The huge explosions damaged towers and palaces and collapsed a portion of the Kremlin wall.

As Napoleon and his army fled Moscow, the Russian army now returned to battle and harass the French. Of the 600,000 soldiers who had marched into Russia, only 30,000 lived to return to France. Many of them died because of the cold weather during their retreat. Because of the Russian victory,

The Bettmann Archive Inc.

Pyotr Ilich Tchaikovsky composed his "1812" overture for the Moscow Exhibition in 1882. This musical work celebrated Russia's victory over the French invasion seventy years earlier.

Czar Alexander I was called the "liberator of Europe."

The famous Russian composer Pyotr (Peter) Ilich Tchaikovsky wrote the "1812" overture to commemorate that year of war and great victory. The music features both the French and the Russian national anthems, and church bells of Moscow ringing in triumph at the end.

In 1905, Russia was defeated by Japan. In the battle of Tsu-Shima, Russia's entire fleet was destroyed (above). A postcard of the era shows Japan's modern army (right).

One of the newer monuments in modern Moscow is the Panorama of the Battle of Borodino, which contains a replica of the great battle. Every day, hundreds of Russian schoolchildren and other citizens visit this monument to learn about Russia's important victory over Napoleon in 1812.

Years of War and Revolution

After Napoleon's defeat, Muscovites returned to rebuild their city. The population then was about 250,000, and Moscow continued to grow. By 1863, there were 350,000 people living in the city, and by 1882, there were 750,000. Finally, by the year 1900, the city's population had risen to one million.

The 1900s have been a time of great upheaval and change in Moscow and in all of Russia. The land has been torn by revolution, changes in government, and civil war. It has been battered by two world wars.

War, of course, is armed conflict between nations. A revolution occurs when people rise up to overthrow

their government, as in the American and French revolutions. A civil war is one in which people of a nation fight each other, as in the American Civil War between the North and South.

In January 1904, war began between Russia and Japan in Manchuria, a part of China that borders Russia. Japan was well prepared to fight. Russia, however, was not, and the war went badly for that country. This caused discontent among a growing number of Russians who were already dissatisfied with the rule of Nicholas II. He had become czar ten years before.

In addition to the war, crop failures in 1904 made food scarce. Many peasants left the countryside for cities, seeking food and jobs in the factories. Working hours in factories were long, wages were low, and general working conditions were miserable.

Early in 1905, workers in St. Petersburg went on strike. On January 22, thousands of them moved toward the Winter Palace with a petition for the czar. The petition asked for better working conditions and government under a constitution instead of rule only by the czar and his advisers. Nicholas II was not at the Winter Palace, but his soldiers were. They fired on the workers, killing at least two hundred of them. Workers called the day Bloody Sunday.

News of Russia's final defeat by Japan in 1905 touched off more strikes and riots. Czar Nicholas II at last agreed that a group of representatives, together called the Duma, would be

On January 22, 1905, protesters marched on the Winter Palace in St. Petersburg to present a petition to the czar. Soldiers opened fire on the marchers killing at least two hundred people. Although the czar was not present, the Russian people blamed him for the heartless actions of his troops.

SovFoto

elected to make laws for Russia. The Duma had little real power, though, and the czar's troops finally crushed the revolution by the people in December 1905.

In 1914, Russia joined England and France in World War I against Germany and Austria-Hungary. This war, too, went badly for Russia, as it lost a million soldiers and met defeat at the hands of German armies. Food again was scarce, and there were riots over bread in St. Petersburg (renamed *Petrograd* during the war) and other cities. The people blamed Czar Nicholas II for the way the war had gone, and another revolution was at hand. On March 15, 1917, Nicholas II gave up his throne and the right to rule. After

Nicholas II created the Duma in response to demands for reform. Although elected by the people, it had no power to make laws.

three hundred years of Romanovs, there would be no more czars of Russia. The Duma became Russia's government.

The people wanted an end to the war, and they wanted food and fuel. The Duma, led by Aleksandr Kerensky, did not meet the people's demands. Russia remained in the war as turmoil spread.

In the meantime, a group of revolutionaries called Bolsheviks planned to take over the government. They were led by Vladimir Ilyich Lenin, who had devoted his life to trying to bring revolution to Russia.

Nicholas II, the last czar to rule the Russians, was removed from power during the revolution of 1917. The czar and his family were imprisoned and later shot to death by soldiers of the Red Army.

The Bolsheviks struck in October 1917, taking control in Petrograd and other cities. By November, they also took over Moscow. Once in control of the government, the Bolsheviks took Russia out of the war and promised food for workers and land for peasants. Later, the Bolsheviks changed their name to the Communist Party.

A bitter civil war that was to last for more than three years now began between the Whites, who opposed communism, and the Reds, as communists were called. Communists had imprisoned Czar Nicholas II and his wife and five children. During the civil war, they had the czar and his family shot to death in the village of Ekaterinburg (now Sverdlovsk), where they had been held.

The civil war ended in 1921 with the Red Army victorious. By then, the capital had been moved back to Moscow. The name of the nation was soon changed from Russia to the Union of Soviet Socialist Republics, and Petrograd was renamed Leningrad.

Early Years of Communism

According to the communist ideal, the government would own all land, factories, and systems of transportation and communication on behalf of the people. There would be no private property. Everyone would work together for the good of all. Each person would give to society according to his ability and receive according to his need. Everyone would have the right to a job and an income, a place to live, an education, and health care paid for by the government.

Under communism, millions of people were better off than they had been under the czars. However, the people had little freedom. They had no voice in government. The Communist Party controlled the government, and eventually nearly everything else, in the Soviet Union. A secret police force made sure that no one spoke out against the party or the government.

Shots echoed in the courtyard of the Winter Palace as Bolsheviks exchanged gunfire with government soldiers during the October revolution.

Lenin died in 1924. A few years later, Joseph Stalin became the leader of the Soviet Union, and he proved to be a cruel and crafty dictator. Stalin decided that peasants should be organized and tightly supervised to produce food, as the Soviet Union built up its industrial strength. The government forced peasants to give up their land and live and work on huge farms called collectives, some of which held as many as fifteen thousand people.

During the 1930s, Stalin set out to wipe out all possible opposition to his

Lenin (left) headed the communist government that took power in 1917. The communists reorganized agriculture into large collective farms, where the high cost of equipment could be shared by many farmers working together (above).

rule. To begin with, he ordered his secret police to round up his enemies. The millions of "enemies"—including peasants who refused to surrender their land—were shot or sent to prison camps in Siberia. By the end of the 1930s, Stalin's power in the Soviet Union had no limits.

At this time, Stalin also began a series of five-year plans. The government set goals of production that workers on farms and in factories were to fulfill. The government also decided the wages that workers would receive and the prices that people would pay for goods that were produced.

The Growth of Moscow Under Stalin

Factory workers in Moscow often led the way in overfulfilling factory production goals. Other workers built many new government, office, and apartment buildings in the city. A new building design appeared in Moscow in the 1930s, called "Stalin Gothic" after Joseph Stalin. Seven skyscrapers of this design were built, and they featured many towers and spires. Today one of them contains dormitories, classrooms, and offices of Moscow University. Another is a hotel.

A new style of architecture called "Stalin Gothic" appeared in the 1930s (above). It was named after Joseph Stalin (right).

29

The Stalin era gave Moscow its 125-mile (200 km) subway system known as the Metro. Electric trains (left) carry passengers between stations that are as large as ballrooms, many brilliantly lit with chandeliers (above).

Moscow's population grew from two million in 1917 to about three million in 1930. To provide transportation for Muscovites, work began on a subway system, called the Metro, in 1932. More than sixty thousand men and women workers and five thousand engineers labored on the project. The underground stations they built are large and brilliantly lit, and each is decorated differently with colored marble, ceramic tiles, stained glass, chandeliers, frosted lamps, and mosaic artwork. A medieval warrior on a white horse adorns the ceiling of the great Komsomolskaya Station. Here, mosaics and paints depict events of the country's military past. This station is dedicated to young workers who helped build the subway.

The Moscow Metro is the most spectacular subway in the world. It carries more than seven million passengers each day on 125 miles (200 km) of track. The commuter trains are called *elektrichka,* and it costs only five *kopeks* to ride them—about a dime in American money. All this was done according to a plan to rebuild and beautify Moscow.

Also as part of this plan, aboveground streets were widened and paved. The main squares of the city—Sverdlov Square, Dzerzhinsky Square, and Revolution Square—were expanded and beautified. New bridges were built. New libraries and many new schools were opened. Large public gardens and parks were designed, and trees and shrubs were planted throughout the city.

In 1935, a major change was made in the Kremlin towers. The two-headed eagles, symbols of the czars, were taken down from their perches on the tower tops. In their place, huge stars made of red glass were mounted on the very tops of the towers. These stars are lit at night and turn with the wind. Whether viewing the Kremlin from a boat on the Moscow River, from Red Square, or from the window of a building, one can see the giant red stars.

When Moscow became the capital of the new Soviet state, the Kremlin became the center of government. In 1935, red stars—the symbol of communism—were set atop the Kremlin's towers.

Novosti / Gamma-Liaison

By the year 1940, Moscow had been the capital of the Soviet Union for twenty years. The population had increased to about four million people. Many new factories were producing goods there, and wages had improved. Social and medical services were available to all. Although working people lived under a harsh dictatorship, their standard of living had gone steadily upward since the revolution. By 1940, however, Europe was once again in the midst of war.

World War II

During the 1930s, Adolf Hitler became dictator of Germany, and he planned to conquer Europe. In 1939, Hitler signed a treaty of friendship with Joseph Stalin and then sent his armies to invade Poland, which lay between Germany and the Soviet Union. England and France then declared war on Germany, and World War II began. Hitler quickly conquered Poland and France. England fought on alone against Germany.

Then, on June 22, 1941, Hitler broke the treaty of friendship with Stalin. In a surprise attack, German tanks and troops crossed into the Soviet Union from Poland. German forces captured numerous Soviet cit-

In 1941, Adolf Hitler ignored his treaty with Stalin and attacked the Soviet Union.

ies, and by the end of 1941, Moscow and Leningrad were under attack. In Moscow, people built 100 miles (161 km) of barricades, barbed wire, and log obstacles against the Germans. As

German warplanes dropped bombs on the city, young people were organized to put out fires.

In the meantime, the Japanese attacked the American naval base at Pearl Harbor, Hawaii. This brought the United States into World War II on the side of England and the Soviet Union, and America supplied both nations with war materials.

During World War II, the Soviets defended their homeland using whatever weapons they could find. Cannons made in 1870 were used to defend the city of Przemysl .

The winter of 1941-1942 was bitterly cold in Moscow. There were shortages of fuel and food, and the German attack continued. The Germans, however, were unprepared for the cold winter. It helped defeat them at Moscow in 1942 just as it had helped defeat Napoleon 130 years before.

By early in 1942, the Soviet army had driven the Germans back from Moscow. Soviet forces continued to attack the Germans and gradually drove them westward into Germany itself. There the Soviets joined English, French, and American troops that had invaded Germany from the west in 1944. World War II ended in Europe in 1945 with total German defeat.

In the Soviet Union, World War II is called the Great Patriotic War. It cost that nation twenty million military and civilian dead. This was more than any other nation lost. Many Soviet cities lay in ruins, and many people were without housing. Schools had to be used as hospitals. Factories could not produce enough goods, and all the people had to do without things they needed. Many of the years after 1945 were spent recovering from the war, as workers in Moscow and elsewhere repaired and rebuilt streets, parks, schools, apartment buildings, houses, stores, and factories.

On September 6, 1947, the government of the Soviet Union awarded Moscow the Order of Lenin, in appreciation of its people's courage during the Great Patriotic War. People filled the streets in celebration, and at night, colored lights beamed up from the Kremlin walls and shone brightly from bridges and high buildings. That day also marked the 800th anniversary of Moscow's beginning. As part of the celebration, the foundation stone was laid for the monument to the city's founder, Prince Yuri Dolgoruki.

World War II cost the Soviet Union the lives of twenty million citizens. Those who fought are still heroes (right). At Moscow's Tomb of the Unknown Soldier, the dead are remembered (below).

Marti / SYGMA

Click / Chicago Ltd. - Karen Sherlock

Postwar Change

The Soviet Union and the United States had fought as allies against Germany in World War II. After the war, though, relations between the two nations turned sour. Aided by the Soviet Union, communist parties seized power in several countries of Eastern Europe. These countries included Hungary, Bulgaria, Czechoslovakia, East Germany, Romania, and Poland. Joseph Stalin insisted that having friendly governments to the west was needed to help prevent another invasion of his country like that by the French in 1812 and by Germans in the two world wars. American leaders pointed out that the new governments in Eastern Europe had not been elected democratically. They believed

that Stalin really meant for the Soviet Union to take over all of Europe. In turn, Stalin believed that the United States wanted to destroy communism in the Soviet Union and elsewhere.

Thus, a period of deep suspicion and distrust known as the Cold War began. During this time, the Soviet Union and the United States both built large weapons systems that included missiles and airplanes with atomic bombs. Although the two countries did not fight battles, they behaved in every other way as though they were enemies.

Khrushchev and Brezhnev

Joseph Stalin died in 1953. Nikita S. Khrushchev took over in the Kremlin as the Soviet Union's new leader. Under Khrushchev, life in the Soviet Union became somewhat more open than it had been under Stalin. The secret police grew less active; writers, artists, and scientists were allowed more freedom of expression; the work-week was shortened to about forty hours; and workers became more free to change jobs.

Leonid I. Brezhnev replaced Khrushchev as Soviet leader in 1964. After that, the Soviet Union gradually became more of a closed society once again, though the harsh days of the Stalin dictatorship did not return. Relations with the United States worsened after the Soviet Union invaded Afghanistan, a small country to the south, in 1979.

In 1980, Moscow became the center of the world's attention as it hosted the Summer Olympic Games. The athletes lived in Olympic Village, a huge complex of eighteen apartment houses, each sixteen stories tall. Most of the main events were held in Lenin Central Stadium on the banks of the Moscow River below Moscow University. Here more than 100,000 people gathered at one time to watch track and field events and soccer games.

More than one billion viewers all over the world watched the games on television, and thousands of tourists came to Moscow for the first time.

In 1980, Moscow hosted the Summer Olympics. Because the Soviets had sent troops to Afghanistan in 1979, the United States refused to send its athletes to compete in the games.

Today, fifteen thousand Muscovites live in what was the Olympic Village.

Because of the Afghanistan invasion, the United States refused to send athletes to the Moscow Games. In return, the Soviet Union did not participate in the 1984 Summer Olympics, which were held in Los Angeles, California.

New Leadership, New Directions

The 1980 Summer Olympics were a bright spot in the lives of Muscovites. Problems within the Soviet Union had been growing, and they became severe in the 1980s.

Of all the problems, those having to do with the production of food and factory goods were the most difficult. Although production had increased over the years, it had not kept up with the needs of the people. The people of Moscow and other cities often had to stand in long lines to buy food and other items. Sometimes, such foods as meat and fruit were not available at all. At other times, it was hard to find things such as soap and certain kinds of clothing. There never seemed to be

Most new apartments in Moscow are cement flat-blocks built to house many hundreds of people (above). Inside, rooms are cramped, and residents have only a few simple furnishings (left).

Mikhail Gorbachev (at left) has had more contact with the Soviet people than did previous leaders. Here, Gorbachev takes time to speak with a worker while touring a Soviet factory.

enough refrigerators, stoves, and other appliances to satisfy demand. In Moscow and other cities, housing remained scarce. Families had to wait for years for apartments large enough for them.

To make matters worse, many new apartments were poorly built. Many goods that factories in Moscow and other Soviet cities produced were of poor quality. Televisions, washing machines, and other appliances often needed repair soon after they were bought. Tractors and other machines for farms also broke down quickly, or did not operate properly from the beginning.

Workers did not seem to care about their jobs any longer. They did not perform well, loafed on the job, and took time off whenever they wished. Production plans went unfulfilled, especially in agriculture. The communist system of five-year plans, with government officials deciding what kinds of and how many goods to produce, was in trouble.

In 1985, the Soviet Union got a new leader. Mikhail S. Gorbachev became general secretary of the Communist Party and leader of the Soviet government. Gorbachev set out to make important changes.

One change had to do with *perestroika,* which means "restructuring" or "making over." The goal of perestroika is to increase farm and factory production and make sure that factories produce goods of high quality. Families on collective farms are now allowed to work more land on their own and keep the income received from selling crops they produce. The idea is to encourage them to produce more food. For factories there is less government planning, and factory owners have a voice in setting production goals. Workers who do not perform well can have their wages reduced or be fired. People in Moscow and other cities are encouraged to begin small businesses of their own to earn extra income.

Another change had to do with *glasnost,* which means "openness." Soviet citizens today are allowed more freedom of expression, including the freedom to criticize the government. They are more free to travel within the Soviet Union and to other countries. Some people who had been put in prison because of their ideas have been freed. The secret police no longer keep such a close watch on everyone.

Gorbachev's economic reforms have allowed individuals to prosper. Many factories are now privately owned (opposite, top). Farm workers are allowed to keep profits from their crops. Sellers offer spices at a farm market (opposite, bottom).

F. Hibon / SYGMA

With the recent political reforms, more women are now visible in the Supreme Soviet, the Soviet Union's ruling body.

Mikhail Gorbachev himself has gone out to mingle with people on the streets and in stores, schools, and factories of Moscow and other cities. He has discussed perestroika and glasnost with them and listened to their ideas.

Openness under Gorbachev has gone further than it did under Nikita Khrushchev. Gorbachev's changes have applied to government as well as to other aspects of Soviet life. Through his changes, the people have greater freedom in choosing their government representatives.

In 1988, the last Soviet troops crossed back over the border between Afghanistan and the Soviet Union. After almost ten years of war, the soldiers returned home.

Elections had been held in the past, but voters had no choice of candidates. They could vote or not vote for the one person the Communist Party presented. Because of Gorbachev's changes, more than one candidate can run for office. In the spring of 1989, voters had choices to make as they voted for members of the Congress of Deputies, which is now part of the lawmaking process. Citizens voted a number of old-guard communists out of office, electing people who were new to government.

Gorbachev also sought good relations between the Soviet Union and other nations. He stopped the war in Afghanistan and brought Soviet troops home. He visited the United States, China, and European countries to discuss ways in which they and the Soviet Union might work together. He also invited leaders of other nations to Moscow for further talks. Under Gorbachev, it appeared that the Cold War might finally come to an end.

WORLD

CITIES

Living in Moscow

In the Soviet Union today, a couple wishing to marry must go through a civil ceremony. That is, a government official must perform the wedding. If they wish, the couple may later be married in a religious ceremony, too.

Most marriages in Moscow take place in the Palace of Weddings. Grooms wear suits; brides wear wedding dresses and carry flowers. One or more other couples act as witnesses. Music plays from a record player as the official lectures the couple briefly on the responsibilities of marriage, pronounces them husband and wife, and congratulates them. The newlyweds then have a reception in the Palace of Weddings, in a restaurant, or in someone's home.

Apartment Life

It is not unusual for newlyweds to live with parents for the first months, as they work their way up the waiting list for a small apartment of their own to rent. Apartment construction in Moscow has not kept up with demand by a growing population.

When children are born, the couple puts their name on a waiting list for a larger apartment. The wait may last several years. A family could buy what is called a cooperative apartment, but these are too expensive for many people.

A typical family of four lives in a small apartment with one bedroom, a living room, a kitchen, and a bathroom. Often four tall buildings—

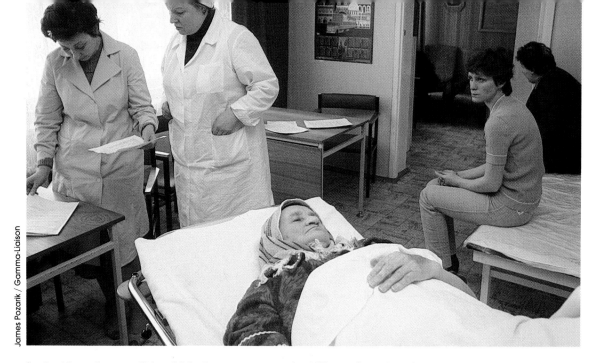

Soviet ideas about traditional jobs for women are quite different from those in other countries. In the Soviet Union, almost all of the medical doctors are women.

forming a square around a large playground area—make up an apartment complex. Next to the playground, there is usually a nursery for babies and children up to three years of age.

Women and Young Children

Most women in the Soviet Union have jobs outside the home. Some women are scientists, doctors, lawyers, college professors, or teachers. Other women are salesclerks, government or office workers, or bus drivers. Few jobs in the Soviet Union are not open to women.

Mothers can take several months off work after a baby is born. When they return to work, they may leave the baby with grandparents during the day, but more often, babies are placed in a nursery. The nursery may be in the apartment complex, at the mother's workplace, or at some other location.

At age three, children go to kindergarten. There they play games, go on field trips, prepare to learn to read, and learn to work together. Most children are in kindergarten, as they were in the nursery, from 7:30 A.M. until 5:30 P.M.

Going to School

Children enter the first grade at age six. In some schools, the students wear uniforms. Boys wear dark blue jackets and pants with white shirts. Girls wear brown dresses with long sleeves and removable collars and cuffs. On most days, they also wear black aprons tied at the waist. White aprons are worn on holidays and other special occasions.

Classes in grades one through four, called the elementary grades, meet six days a week. School lasts for 4½ hours Monday through Friday and for a shorter time on Saturday. The school day begins at 8:30A.M. as students listen to the news of the day over radio or television and then do some warm-up exercises. They then go to classes in which they study art, arithmetic, language, physical education, and music. In grade four, nature study and history are added, and beginning at that grade, students have a different teacher for each subject.

Soviet grade schools teach classes in gymnastics as well as academic subjects (above). Like students everywhere, schoolchildren in Moscow have homework assignments to turn in to their teachers (below).

Grades five through eight are the intermediate grades. School is now in session thirty hours a week. Students have language, botany, geography, history, geometry, algebra, zoology, physics, literature, chemistry, anatomy, and physiology. Students begin the study of English or some other foreign language in grade five. Each class in the intermediate grades, as in the elementary grades, lasts forty-five minutes.

Late in the morning, intermediate-grade students have a brief break for a light snack of milk or juice and bread and cheese. Classes end at 2 P.M., after which students perform their school chores, cleaning chalkboards, sweeping floors, taking out wastepaper, and watering plants. They then have a large meal at school at about 3 P.M.

After school, students may remain at school to begin their homework for the following day. Elementary school students have about two hours of homework each night. Intermediate students have even more. Often, students put their homework aside for later and participate in games or other activities that the schools offer. Students may also take part in Young

Pioneer activities in clubhouses scattered throughout Moscow.

Millions of boys and girls between ages nine and fifteen belong to the Young Pioneers and wear the Young

The Young Pioneers is a popular after-school organization for young people. The Pioneer activities teach communist politics.

Pioneer uniform of red cap and scarf. The organization exists to help schools teach young people patriotism and loyalty to the Communist Party, and it sponsors community projects and many other activities. At clubhouses, members take part in athletics, games of chess, model building, scientific projects, sewing, arts and crafts, folk dancing, drama, or auto mechanics.

Students listen with headphones to recordings of spoken English in this foreign language class at a Moscow secondary school.

After grade eight, some students go on to grades nine and ten of a secondary school. There they study mathematics, science, languages, social science, and literature and have classes in physical education. Secondary schools prepare students for colleges or universities, if they wish to go after passing examinations. Students who do not go to secondary school go to a trade or technical school after grade eight. In these schools, students learn skills that will be useful to jobs in agriculture, industry, engineering, and other areas.

Family Activities

Nearly every family in Moscow has a television. Each republic has its own station, and the Moscow station broadcasts throughout the nation. Programs in Moscow are beamed from a thin tower rising 1,762 feet (537 meters) into the air, standing three times taller than the Washington Monument in Washington, D.C. Televised soccer and ice hockey games are the favorites with many people, and there are also television programs on news, science, travel, health, and music. Cartoon shows are a favorite among children, and people of all ages like dramatized fairy tales.

Moscow has many parks, of which Gorky, Sakolnicky, and Vorontsovo parks are the best known. Families enjoy the parks on Sundays and holidays for boating, swimming, picnicking, listening to band music, fishing, or just sitting on benches or lying on the grass. During the winter months, people use the parks for skating and cross-country skiing. There are two jumps for skiers on the embankment in front of Moscow University.

An outing at a Moscow park might mean an afternoon of painting with watercolors or a cruise around a park lagoon on a paddleboat.

Mushroom hunting is another favorite family activity among Muscovites. In season, families ride trains to wooded areas on the city's outskirts to gather mushrooms that will be fried, boiled, baked, pickled, or eaten raw over the weeks to come.

Grocery shopping is almost an everyday event, for most families do not have refrigerators large enough to keep much food for any length of time. Women often grocery shop on the way home from work, which makes their day away from home longer. In most families, everyone depends on the women to make the evening meal as well.

Families buy food, clothing, and furniture on Kalinin Prospect or Gorky Street, two main shopping areas. They

Moscow has no supermarkets. Shoppers buy their groceries at stores which specialize in a single type of food. Above is a vegetable market.

can also go to the large, government-owned department store, GUM. With its fountains, chandeliers, and arches, GUM is the Moscow version of a shopping mall. The many small shops within the larger store offer goods of all kinds. Another well-known shopping place is *Detskii Mir*—which means "Children's World"—in the center of Moscow. Here families find school uniforms and all kinds of children's clothing.

Shopping for many things in Moscow must be on an "if you see it, buy it" basis. Many household goods, articles of clothing, and other items remain scarce.

More than 150 individual shops line the three stories of walkways inside Moscow's GUM department store. GUM faces Red Square.

51

Novosti / Gamma-Liaison

Moscow young people are very much like young people everywhere. Here, concertgoers enjoy the performance of a Soviet rock group in a city park.

Teenagers in Moscow participate in family activities, but they also like to spend much of their time with people of their own age. Teenagers in Moscow are much the same as they are the world over. They dress in T-shirts and jeans, listen and dance to rock music, and flock to rock concerts. Older teens often congregate on Arbat Street, which has been the center of a Moscow marketplace for seven hundred to eight hundred years. There they drink soda or coffee, talk, and watch artists at work.

New Year's

The Russian people celebrate New Year's much the way people in western countries celebrate Christmas. New Year's is the highlight of the year for families. Fir and balsam trees are decorated in homes, in office buildings, and on the streets of Moscow. *Deduska Moroz,* Grandfather Frost, always comes with presents for the children.

Children also enjoy puppet shows and plays on New Year's. A favorite fairy tale drama is *Tsarevnaya Ligushka (The Frog Princess).*

Vacation Time

Summer is vacation time for Muscovites, and most families are eager to get out of the hot city to the cooler and more pleasant countryside. Many have *dachas,* or summer cottages, located along lakes or rivers or in wooded areas. Some dachas have several rooms and are luxurious. Only well-to-do people can afford them. Most families, however, are content with simple, small cabins without plumbing or electricity. They are prepared to rough it for a chance to enjoy a vacation in a different environment.

Today there is a struggle for control of land near Moscow on which dachas can be built. The city government wants to preserve the land for public recreation. Many citizens want to keep it open for private cabins.

WORLD

CITIES

Moscow and the Arts

A city mirrors the talents of its people, and Moscow has produced many significant writers, musicians, and artists. Their work and spirit are everywhere in the city. Schoolchildren learn about them, and citizens and tourists enjoy their work. The people of Moscow remember their great artists in monuments, exhibits, and performances.

Architecture and Monuments

The word *architecture* refers to the way buildings are designed and constructed. Moscow has some remarkable architecture in its churches and other buildings.

One example is St. Basil's Cathedral on Red Square, with its colorful onion-shaped domes. St. Basil's is more than four hundred years old. It was built during Ivan the Terrible's rule to celebrate a military victory.

Another example of Moscow's fine architecture is the Cathedral of the Archangel Michael, where several czars are buried. Most of the churches that are still standing are made of stone, and domes were often overlaid in gold. This church architecture is uniquely Russian.

Other designs for Moscow's early buildings included ornate towers and archways and steep, tent-shaped roofs. Buildings from these early years are decorated with tile and brick designs. Many examples of this style of architecture still stand, having survived the

great fire of 1812 that led to Napoleon's defeat.

After the fire, many buildings in the city were rebuilt, but in a new style. It was called neoclassical, or "new classical." This style copied the architecture of ancient Greece and Rome. Neoclassical buildings have tall pillars, broad steps, rounded domes, and grand entrances. The Bolshoi Theater is one neoclassical building in Moscow. Examples of this kind of building can also be seen in Washington, D.C.

Moscow is also a city of monuments. One monument, for example, honors Prince Yuri Dolgoruki, who began the city. Another, in the shape of a rocket, honors Soviet achievements in space. Then there is the Panorama of the Battle of Borodino.

The best-known and most-visited monument is Lenin's tomb, on Red Square. There, the remains of the first leader of the Soviet Union lie in a glass-enclosed, airtight case. Soviet leaders today view parades in Red Square from atop Lenin's tomb.

Operas and ballets have been performed in the Bolshoi Theater in Moscow (top) since 1776. The Kosmos Monument (bottom) honors Soviet accomplishments in space exploration.

Painting

The best collections of Russian and Soviet art are to be found at the Tretyakov Gallery and the Pushkin Museum of Fine Art. At these museums, visitors can see all kinds of Muscovite art from ancient to modern times.

Most early paintings were icons. Icons are religious images painted on wooden panels. Many icons depict Jesus, saints, and other biblical figures. They were the main form of art in Russia for hundreds of years.

People lit candles and prayed before icons, and most families kept one in a niche at home to show devotion to God. Some people believed that icons could work miracles. Most icons were not signed by the artists, but it is known that most of these artists were monks of the Russian Orthodox Church.

In the 1700s, Russian artists began to paint other kinds of scenes. They painted the Russian countryside, scenes from Moscow's streets, portraits of famous Muscovites, still lifes, and scenes from Russian history and legends. Visitors to Moscow's art museums can see examples of all of these types of paintings.

The Andrey Rublyov Museum is named for one of Russia's greatest painters of icons. The museum specializes in these religious artworks.

Click / Chicago LTD. - Jadwigg Lopez

Museums

The treasures of Moscow are preserved for all to see in about eighty museums. They cover almost every subject one can think of—art, literature, music, theater, history, science, and technology.

One of the oldest and richest museums is the Armory Palace in the Kremlin. There, visitors can see armor and weapons used by soldiers who fought the Mongols and Tatars long ago. They can admire beautiful gold and silver jewelry made by Russian crafts people hundreds of years ago. They can even see the thrones on which czars sat. The thrones are richly decorated with jewels and ivory.

St. Basil's Cathedral (above), built in 1552 by Ivan the Terrible, today contains a museum. Poet and novelist Boris Pasternak (left) received the 1958 Nobel Prize for Literature.

The State Historical Museum is part of St. Basil's on Red Square. There, visitors can see tools used by the ancestors of the Russians who lived in prehistoric times. This museum also displays important documents that tell the story of Russia's history. One hall exhibits the personal belongings and weapons used by heroes of the 1917 revolution.

Literature

Many of Russia's greatest writers called Moscow their home. Aleksandr (Alexander) Pushkin, who lived from 1799 to 1837, is recognized as an outstanding genius of Russian literature. He wrote poetry, plays, and stories before his early death in a duel. Of his city he wrote, "Moscow—to Russian hearts how much it means! How many memories [it] redeems!"

The poet Mikhail Lermontov (1814-1841) entered Moscow University at the age of sixteen, then left and joined the military. When Pushkin was killed, Lermontov wrote a poem blaming corruption in the czar's court for his death. Lermontov was forced into exile, and it was then that he did his greatest writing. He said, "Moscow is my sweet home, and I will love it as long as I live."

Fyodor Dostoevsky (1821-1881) was the son of a Moscow doctor. He wrote such important novels as *Notes from the Underground, Crime and Punishment, The Idiot,* and *The Brothers Karamazov,* in which he dealt with corruption, tyranny, guilt, and freedom. Dostoevsky was sent to prison for some of his writing.

Leo Tolstoy (1828-1910) was a member of Moscow's aristocracy, or wealthy upper class. His family estate is now a national museum. Tolstoy's most famous novels are *War and Peace* and *Anna Karenina.* Both are about the lives of people in the aristocracy.

Anton Chekhov (1860-1904) was another important Russian writer. Many of Chekhov's plays and stories show what Russian life was like in the late 1800s. His works examine the middle-class Russian people, often capturing the gloominess of their lives under the czars. Chekhov came to Moscow when he was nineteen to study medicine. He began writing as a way to earn more money for his family, which, because of his father's ill health, was often poor. However, even after finishing medical school, Chekhov continued to write. Eventually, he devoted himself to it. Some of his works include *The Sea Gull, The Three Sisters,* and *The Cherry Orchard.*

Like Dostoevsky, some more recent writers have run into trouble with government officials because they criticized the government or offended it in some other way. Such writers include Boris Pasternak (1890-1960) and Alexander Solzhenitsyn (born in 1918). In 1958, Pasternak won the Nobel Prize for his novel *Doctor Zhivago,* which dealt sympathetically with upper-class people around the time of the 1917 revolution. The novel could be published only in other countries until 1987, when Soviet officials finally allowed it to appear in the Soviet Union. Solzhenitsyn spent time in a labor camp in Siberia and wrote about his experiences there. The government took away his citizenship and forced him to leave the Soviet Union. Solzhenitsyn now lives in the United States. Most of his books still have not been published in his native country.

compositions performed are by Russian composers of the nineteenth and twentieth centuries, such as Mikhail Glinka, Modest Mussorgsky, Aleksandr Borodin, Nikolay Rimsky-Korsakov, Anton Rubinstein, Pyotr Ilich Tchaikovsky, Sergey Rachmaninoff, Igor Stravinsky, and Sergey Prokofiev.

Russian music often includes themes from folk tales, which are popular with Muscovites and tourists alike. You may recognize some titles of Russian compositions: *The Nutcracker, Firebird, Pictures at an Exhibition, Overture to Romeo and Juliet, Peter and the Wolf,* and *Swan Lake.*

Classical ballet, which has been performed in Moscow for more than three hundred years, is the performing art for which Russians are best known. Famous Russian artists of the ballet in the nineteenth and twentieth centuries have included Anna Pavlova (1881-1931), Vaslav Nijinsky (1890-1950), Rudolf Nureyev (1938-), and Mikhail Baryshnikov (1948-). The last two now live and work in the United States, where Baryshnikov has directed the American Ballet Theater.

A new generation of writers, artists, and musicians may soon begin to flourish in Moscow should glasnost continue to progress. Writers in Moscow are already speaking out about the important political and social changes taking place in their country.

Soviet composer Sergey Prokofiev (top) is famous for his symphonic tale Peter and the Wolf. *Ballet dancers Rudolf Nureyev (left) and Mikhail Baryshnikov (right) now live in America.*

Music and Dance

The concert halls of Moscow are filled each night. Some of the finest

WORLD CITIES

Past and Future

Moscow began as a tiny settlement in the 1100s. By the beginning of the 1900s, Moscow had become the cultural center of Russia but not much more. It was a very big town, even then, but it was poor and many people were not educated. The government was in disarray and about to crumble. Few foreigners visited the city, and the world cared little for what went on there.

Today, however, Moscow is a leading world city. It is the center of power in the Soviet Union just as Washington, D.C., is in the United States. In fact, Moscow can be considered a center of power for all of Eastern Europe. Most of the communist countries there are strongly influenced by what goes on in Moscow. Beyond that, however, Moscow is a symbol of the ideas and intent of the Soviet leaders and people. The same is true of Washington, D.C., which is a symbol of the United States. When you watch the news on television, the commentator might say, "Washington has taken steps to reach an agreement" or "Moscow will make an offer to Washington next week." Both Washington and Moscow represent the spirit and deeds of a nation.

Moscow's growth has been closely linked to that of the Soviet Union. The city's rise to a world-leading position came as the nation expanded and became one of the world's largest. By the time Russia became the Union of

May Day is celebrated in Moscow each year with a parade of armed forces.

Soviet Socialist Republics, the nation covered one-sixth of the earth's land surface. From its western border in Europe, the Soviet Union stretches for nearly 6,000 miles (9,656 km) across part of Europe and all of Siberia to the Kamchatka Peninsula on the Pacific Ocean. The greatest distance north and south is 3,200 miles (5,150 km). A person traveling from west to east in the Soviet Union crosses eleven time zones.

War and revolution swirled around and within Moscow over the years, particularly during the twentieth century. With the last of the czars overthrown by revolution in 1917, hopes grew that a new society would develop. These hopes were dashed by the harsh rule of Joseph Stalin, which proved to be more oppressive than any known under the czars.

After a great loss of life in World War II, Muscovites and other Soviet citizens rebuilt. Then, having recovered from the war, with the rule of Stalin in the past, the people faced another problem. The communist system, in which many had once had great faith, had nearly ground to a halt.

New ideas and new directions were needed, and a new leader, Mikhail Gorbachev, supplied them. Some years will have to pass, however, before anyone will know just how well glasnost and perestroika will work out. In any case, no one doubts that, as the nation's capital, Moscow is leading the way in whichever direction the country moves.

Moscow: Historical Events

1147 Prince Yuri Dolgoruki builds a fort on the banks of the Moscow River. He is considered to be the founder of the city of Moscow.

1237-
1240 The Mongols conquer Russia.

1326 The head of the Russian Orthodox Church moves to Moscow, making the city the religious center of Russia. The first white stone church is built for him.

1380 Grand Prince Dmitri defeats the Mongols in the Battle of Kulikovo near the Don River.

1479 The Cathedral of the Assumption (also called Dormition) is completed in the Kremlin.

1480 Ivan III stops Mongol control by refusing to pay taxes.

1547 Ivan IV is the first Russian ruler to be crowned czar.

1555 Muscovy Trading Company begins trade between England and Russia.

1584 Ivan IV dies.

1613 Michael Romanov becomes the first Romanov czar.

1682 Peter the Great becomes czar.

1700 By this year, Moscow is the capital of a thriving empire.

1703 Peter the Great begins construction of a new capital city to be known as St. Petersburg (now Leningrad).

1712 St. Petersburg is declared capital of Russia and remains capital until 1917.

1725 Peter the Great dies.

1755 Moscow University is founded.

1812 Napoleon attacks Russia. French and Russian armies meet at the village of Borodino.

1825 There is an uprising against the czar.

1861 Alexander II frees all the serfs.

1905 Japan defeats Russia in the Russo-Japanese War. A revolution forces Nicholas II to form a Duma.

1917 Nicholas II is overthrown during a revolution. The communists seize power with V.I. Lenin as dictator.

1918 Moscow becomes the capital of the Soviet Union. Nicholas II and his family are executed.

1922 Joseph Stalin becomes general secretary of the Communist Party.

1932 Work on the Moscow subway, the Metro, begins.

1941 In June, the German army invades the Soviet Union.

1945 World War II ends, leaving Soviet industry in ruins and twenty million Soviets dead.

1953 Stalin dies. Nikita S. Khrushchev becomes head of the Communist Party.

1964 Leonid I. Brezhnev becomes Soviet leader.

1980 The Summer Olympic Games are held in Moscow. The United States does not participate.

1982 Yuri V. Andropov becomes head of the Communist Party.

1984 Konstantin U. Chernenko becomes head of the Communist Party.

1985 Mikhail S. Gorbachev becomes the Communist Party leader. He announces new policies of openness (*glasnost*) and restructuring (*perestroika*).

Moscow

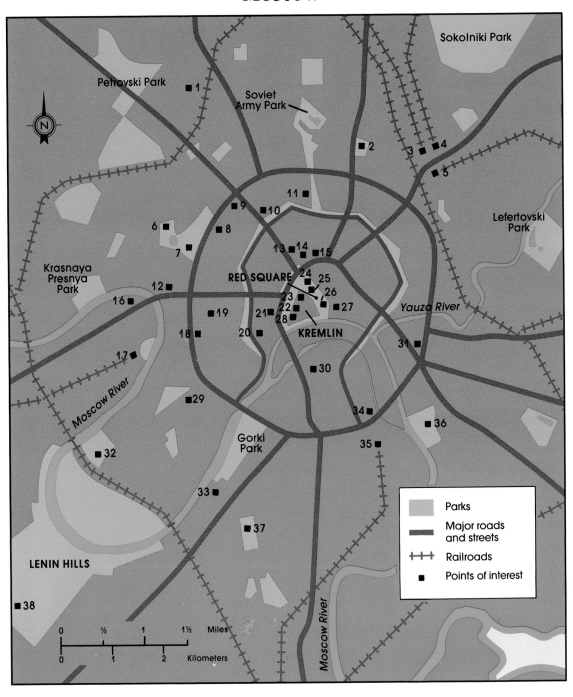

Petrovski Park

Soviet Army Park

Sokolniki Park

1

2

3 4

5

Lefertovski Park

11

9 10

6

8

7

13 14 15

Krasnaya Presnya Park

RED SQUARE 24 25

12

23 26

16

19 21 22 27

18 20 28

Yauza River

KREMLIN

31

17

30

29

34

36

Moscow River

35

Gorki Park

32

33

Parks

Major roads and streets

Railroads

Points of interest

37

LENIN HILLS

38

| 0 | ½ | 1 | 1½ | Miles |

| 0 | 1 | 2 | Kilometers |

Moscow River

Map Key

Moscow Almanac

Location: Latitude—55.5° north. Longitude—37.1° east.

Climate: Continental. Average January temperature—14°F (-10°C). Average July temperature—61°F (16° C). Average annual precipitation—22 inches (56 cm).

Land Area: 339 sq. miles (878 sq. km).

Population: City proper—8,714,000 people. Metropolitan area—same. World ranking—16. Population density—25,705 persons/sq. mile.

Major Airports: Sheremetyevo, Bykovo, Domodedovo, and Vnukovo airports handle over 3,000,000 passengers a year.

Colleges/Universities: 75 colleges, universities, and other institutions of higher learning, including Moscow State University and the Soviet Academy of Sciences.

Media: Newspapers—main newspapers are *Pravda* and *Izvestia*. Radio—1 station: Radio Moscow (broadcasts on 4 channels). Television—1 station: Central Television Studios (broadcasts on 2 channels).

Major Buildings: Czar's Bell Tower—320 feet (97 m). Moscow State University Science Building—37 stories, approximately 410 feet (125 m). Seventh Heaven Restaurant—1,105 feet (337 m). Ostankio TV Tower—1,750 feet (533 m).

Ports: The Southern River Station, Kiev Station, and Northern River Station.

Transportation: Moscow's subway system, called the Metro, has 93 miles (150 km) of track.

Interesting Fact: The world's largest bell is located in Moscow.

Index